Flavours
of Kerala

Flavours of Kerala
Photography & Concept: Salim Pushpanath
Photography Technical Advisor: Anil Kumar K
Text & Recipe: Hena Jacob
Design: Shaji Joseph & Moncy K John
Production Co-ordinator: Thomas Kurian
Images Scanned by: Brijilal
Reproduction by: Colortone Process Pvt. Ltd., India.
Food Stylist (Cover) : Roshna Kader

Printed and bound by Times Offset (M) Sdn Bhd, Malaysia

ISBN 81-88000-07-8

Published by Salim Pushpanath
DEE BEE INFO PUBLICATIONS
"Pushpanath" Malloossery, Kottayam - 686 041. Kerala, India.
Tel: 00 481 2391429, 2302799.
Email: salimpushpanath@gmail.com
www.salimpushpanath.com

Printed in Malaysia

Price: RS. 395/=

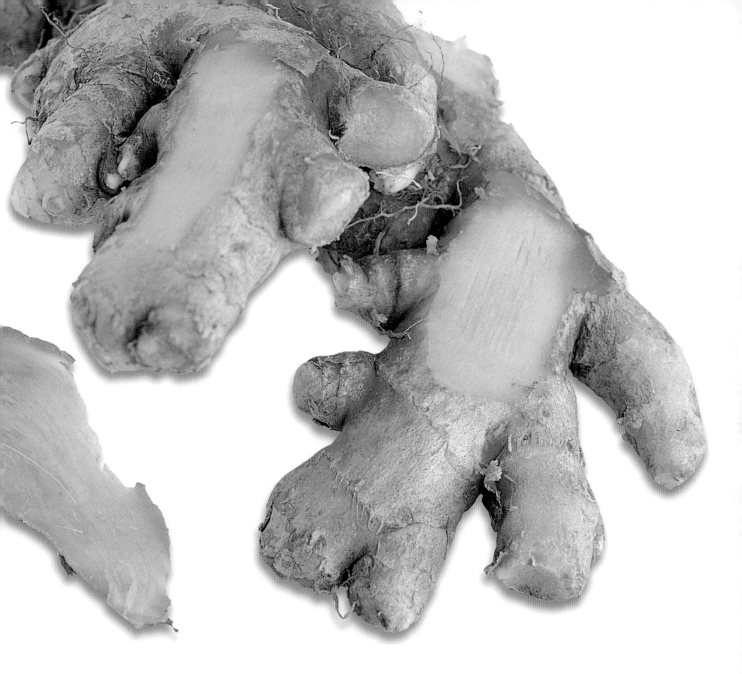

Recipe **Hena Jacob**   Photography **Salim Pushpanath**

INTRODUCTION

Kerala - or the *"land of coconuts"* - as the name denotes is indeed unique in many ways when compared to the other states and union territories that together constitute the Republic of India. One of the primary reasons for this is a her geographical location - situated as she is on the south-western seaboard of the subcontinent with the Arabian Sea in the West and hedged -in by the towering Western Ghats (mountain ranges) on her western border. The undulating shoreline — about 600 square kilometres long — has many a natural harbour and the Southwest Monsoon, which lashes the State every year contributes 73 percent of the 300 mm annual rainfall ensuring that Kerala stays an evergreen tropical paradise around the year. The forty four rivers that flow down from the Western Ghats form an intricate network of canals, lagoons and backwaters leaving fertile alluvial banks in there wake with forty two of them emptying into the Arabian Sea. The plains have lush green paddy fields fringed by lofty coconut palms that give way to expansive Rubber Plantations along the foot hills leading to widespread Tea Gardens, Coffee Estates and extensive cultivation of Spices such as Cardamom, Cloves, Pepper etceteras along the upper reaches of the Ghats.

The Southwest Monsoon is a huge water-laden wind mass that travels for months across the Ocean and opens up over Kerala around the month of June. It not only influences the flora and fauna here but was also primarily responsible for bringing in seafarers from lands as far away as China in the Far East, Persia in the Middle East, countries along the East Coast of Africa and even European countries since time immemorial. This was because ships of yesteryears relied mainly on the direction and force of winds and thus Kerala was the natural destination for eastbound vessels. Around 3000 BC itself, cotton from Kerala was much sought after in Egypt. Jews have been here since the first century AD and they even have a synagogue built in the 16th century AD that is the oldest in the Commonwealth. Marco Polo landed on her shores between 1293 and 1294. Vasco da Gama's fleet *Sao Gabriel,* arrived here on May 20th 1498 having set sail from Port Milindi, off the Kenyan Coast in East Africa — of course guided in by the Southwest Monsoon.

Hinduism, Jainism and Buddhism were the major religions in the state till Saint Thomas, the apostle landed on her shores in AD 52, to spread the Christian Gospel. About a hundred years later, Malik-Ibn-Dinar, a disciple of Prophet Mohammed introduced Islam to Kerala and built the first Mosque in the country in AD 643. The overwhelming Syrian influence in traditional Kerala Churches is attributed to the arrival of about seventy families from Syria led by Thoma of Canan, between AD 200 and AD 400. However, around AD 550 - AD 800, the Arabs had a virtual monopoly of trade with Kerala resulting in the spread of Islam and the gradual decline of Jainism and Buddhism. The major religions during that period were Hinduism, Islam and Christianity.

In the 15th century, frustrated by the Arab monopoly of the Spice trade, the Europeans led by Portugal established supremacy on the shores of Kerala and ruled her shores for about 150 years. The Dutch arrived in the year 1600 and set up the Dutch East India Company and were even successful in driving the Portuguese entirely from Kerala. However in 1741, the Dutch suffered a decisive defeat at the hands of Raja Marthanda Varma and had to eventually leave. Although both the Portuguese and the Dutch plundered Kerala, not only did they introduce cash crops such as Rubber, Papaya, Tapioca and Pineapple to her shores but they also brought with them advanced techniques in agriculture, salt farming and dyeing.

Ironically it was the arrival of the British, (AD 1700 - AD 1947) after driving out Tippu Sultan the invading Maharaja from Mysore that brought hegemony over Kerala. They ruled Kerala with a iron hand suppressing rebellions, introducing English education, modern medicine, the railways, Tea/Coffee plantations and constructing bridges, dams, reservoirs etceteras until India's independence. The modern state of Kerala came into being on November 1st, 1956.

With a rich and vibrant ancient culture greatly influenced by civilisations from almost every corner of the globe down the ages, Kerala is indeed the proverbial melting pot. Close interaction with traders, missionaries and colonists had an indelible impact on the local culture, lifestyle and outlook and is best exemplified in the native cuisine here which is indeed a pot pour ri of exotic preparations unique to this land. The freshest marine food, coconut and a slew of spices are often the main ingredients that lend Kerala Cuisine its very own flavour that is natural as well as nourishing.

Kerala is India's only 100 percent literate state and people of all faiths and religion live in perfect harmony with one another. This is probably because they were beneficiaries of an odd trinity - progressive rulers, a strong Christian school system and later communist led governments. According to the National Geographic Traveller magazine - *"Kerala stands out as the Mount Everest of social development - there is no place like it."* Yet a visit to Kerala gives the impression of a place that seems to dwell in a time warp, where sleek canoes still cruise the backwaters, people dress elegantly in white and the pace of life dignified. The most intriguing aspect of this land is that everyday life especially in the rural settings along the banks of her waterways continues to chug along at a leisurely pace.

The coconut tree is still treasured and every inch of the palm is ingeniously used. Climbing the palm for plucking the nuts; tapping the tree for toddy — a heady extract; making coir from the husk of the nut; extracting oil from the dried flesh of the nut; even using the trunks as make-shift bridges across canals etceteras are just some of the ways that the coconut palm is indigenously used even today. Rice is still cultivated and harvested like in ester years and most of the cultivation along the backwaters in the Kuttanadan region is still done below sea level using dykes. Fishing, especially in the rivers and backwaters are done by hand-casting nets and by setting booby traps made of cane apart from of course angling and spearing. The potter still works his wheel to make beautiful earthen clay pots (traditional red fish curry is only made in them). The only tangible difference is that trucks do the transporting unlike 100 years back when giant "Kettuvallams" or 70 feet long roomy barges ruled the Keralan waterways. The marine delicacies such as prawns, lobsters, pearl-spot (*Karimeen*) especially from the backwaters have a distinct flavour and the manner in which these are traditionally cooked only enhances its taste. Thankfully lack of any major industries in Kerala has helped conserve the environment more or less intact and the waterways of Kerala are relatively free of pollutants.

The utensils commonly used for cooking in Kerala play a major role in determining not only the taste but also the nutritive value of the dishes. Earthen clay pots and utensils of terracotta, bamboo, brass, bronze, copper and even banana leaves are used for the making of these dishes. Utensils such as *mann chatti, palappa chatti, uruli, varpu, puttu kudam* etceteras have unique aesthetic designs. Every recipe listed in this book is authentic and is exactly how the author makes them for her family and friends. The recommended cooking medium for all recipes listed here, is coconut oil as it gives a distinct flavour to the dishes. The basic ingredients may seem all the same and they often are. However, quantities and the manner in which they are added make all the difference.

Bon Appétit!

Acknowledgements

This book would never have been possible without the constant support extended to me by my mother and mother-in-law and I wish to thank them wholeheartedly for all their help and encouragement. Every recipe has been tested live at home and was approved unanimously by my most ardent critics -husband Kitchu, and children Siddharth and Gautham. I would like to especially thank Salim Pushpanath who not only gave me an opportunity to publish the recipes but also waited patiently while I broke deadlines one after another to complete the manuscript.

Hena Jacob

I would like to express my sincere gratitude to Mr.George Dominic who inspired me to take up photography as a profession, the directors of CGH who gave me an opportunity to get the dishes photographed at their facility, Mr.Jose Varkey, Corporate Chef - CGH who was the inspiration behind this venture, Mr.Shaik Asif Ali, Executive Chef - Casino Hotel, Kochi who took great pains in trying out each of the dishes and last but not the least - the unstinting assistance extended by Majo Mathew and Subin Michael.

I would also like to thank Mr. Anil Kumar K who was in many ways my guiding spirit rather than just a technical consultant and Mr.Thomas Kurian for the extraordinary lengths he went to in extending his unconditional support and invaluable inputs.

Salim Pushpanath

SHTEW (STEW)

Preparation Time: 10-15 min. Cooking Time: 15-20 min. Serves: 4-6

Shtew is a tangy curry often served with 'appams' as a starter dish especially for Syrian Christian feasts. Easy to make and compatible with just about everything; this is also a very popular breakfast accompaniment. Lightly garnished with spices and thickened with freshly extracted coconut milk, the shtew is often an instant hit with even first-timers. There are lots of subtle variations to preparing shtew, but this is the one I make at home for the family.

PACHAKKARY SHTEW (VEGETABLE STEW)

Ingredients:

Mixed Vegetables	: 1½ cups of cubed carrot, green peas & beans
Potatoes	: 2 medium-sized; peeled and cubed
Ghee	: 1 teaspoon
Coconut oil	: ¼ cup or 50 ml.
Onions	: 3 medium-sized; thinly sliced
Curry leaves	: 1½ stalk
Coconut milk	: 1 cup first extraction (thick) &1½ cup second extraction (thin)
Green chillies	: 6 sliced or slit
Black pepper powder	: 1 teaspoon.
Ginger	: 5 cm (1 in) cleaned and finely chopped
Garlic	: 4 cloves
Cinnamon stick	: 2½ cm (1 in) piece
Cloves	: 3
Cardamom	: 1 pod

Method of preparation:

- Heat the oil and ghee in a heavy-bottomed pan; and. sauté the crushed spices for 1 minute
- Sauté the onions lightly till it becomes transparent
- Add the mixed vegetables, potatoes, powdered pepper and sauté
- Pour in the thin coconut milk bring to boil
- Reduce the heat and simmer for about 10 minutes till potatoes are tender and ready to split
- Add the thick coconut milk, salt to taste and remove from stove
- Transfer to a serving dish and garnish with curry leaves and powdered cardamom

IRACHI SHTEW (MEAT STEW)

Irachi shtew is prepared in exactly the same manner as above, except that the quantity of mixed vegetables and potatoes may be reduced by about half and 450 g (1 lb.) of cubed meat (Chicken, Mutton or Beef) maybe added instead. The meat is however half-cooked with a dash of pepper and salt usually in a pressure cooker.

PUTTU (STEAMED RICE-CAKE)

Preparation Time: 30-45 min. Cooking Time: 10min. Serves: 3-4

Puttu is a wonderful main dish for breakfast. Easy to make and compatible with everything from ripe bananas to red fish curry this oil-free and healthy dish is made using a unique 2-piece vessel called a puttu-kudam & puttu-kutti. The former is a round-bottomed boiling vessel and the latter is the detachable cylindrical head of either bamboo or aluminium. Puttu made in this type of vessel has a symmetrical shape. If the vessel is not available the same can be made in a steamer also.

Ingredients:

Rice flour (puttu podi)	: 2 cups
Coconut	: 1 cups (grated)
Water	: ¾ cup
Salt	: To taste

Method of preparation:

- Wet or moisten the rice flour, add salt and set apart for ½ hour
- Grind the wet rice flour for a couple of seconds
- Bring water to boil in the puttu-kudam
- Add a tablespoon of coconut
- Top it with 2 tablespoons of rice flour
- Repeat the above alternating method till the puttu-kutti is full
- Take care not to press-in the mixture too tightly
- Cover the puttu-kutti and place on the puttu-kudam
- Cook for 5 minutes after steam starts coming out of puttu-kutti
- Transfer to serving dish & serve hot

19

IDIYAPPAM (STEAMED STRING HOPPERS)

Preparation Time: 15-20 min. Cooking Time: 10min. Serves: 5-6

Idiyappam is yet another delightful dish usually served for breakfast. Pressing the prepared rice flour through what is locally referred to as a sevanazhi gives them a unique shape. However, these can also be made with a potato ricer. These artfully designed string hoppers topped with grated coconut goes well with vegetable/meat stew and just about any curry dish with gravy. My children love them best with just plain milk and a dash of sugar.

Ingredients:

Fine rice flour	: 2 cups
Coconut	: ½ cup (grated)
Water	: 3½ cups
Butter	: 1 teaspoon
Salt	: To taste
Banana leaves	: Cut into 10cm squares

Method of preparation:

- Add salt to water and bring to boil
- Add the rice flour to the boiling water
- Stir well and set apart from the stove
- When the mixture cools down, add the butter and knead well
- Brush the banana leaves lightly with butter
- Sprinkle a spoonful of grated coconut on the leaves
- Press the kneaded mixture through the sevanazhi on to the banana leaves in a circular motion
- Place the leaves in a steamer for 10 minutes
- Remove the banana leaves by flipping the hoppers on to the serving dish

Note: These can also be made in idli moulds if banana leaves are unavailable

ETHAKA APPAM (FRIED BANANA 'N' BATTER)

Preparation Time: 15-20 min. Cooking Time: 10min. Serves: 5-6

Ethaka Appam is a traditional snack popular all over Kerala. They are easy to make and are very tasty especially if the bananas are of the organically grown variety. Please note that the bananas should be ripe yet not overly so. Usually served with tea in the afternoons, they are very popular with children when they get back from school.

Ingredients:

Ripe bananas	: 4 nos.
Flour (Maida)	: 1 cup
Salt	: ¼ teaspoon
Sugar	: 2 teaspoon
Coconut oil	: 2 cups
Water	: 1 cups

Method of preparation:

- Mix the flour, with salt, sugar and water to make the batter
- Peel the bananas and slice into thin pieces
- Heat the oil in a heavy pan
- Dip the sliced bananas in the batter
- Deep-fry till they turn golden brown
- Transfer to serving dish

PAL-APPAM (LACY RICE-CAKE 'N' COCONUT MILK)

Preparation Time: 7-8 hours. Cooking Time: 10 min. Serves: 6-7

Pal-Appam is a soft white lacy rice-cake with crispy brown edges. Traditionally Pal-Appams are made using a shallow wrought-iron wok called an appam-chatti. But a shallow bottom non-stick wok works just as well and if you are using one you need not apply oil on it. Usually served as a starter dish for formal get-togethers it is also a popular breakfast dish and is served with vegetable/meat stew. It also tastes wonderful with thick coconut milk with a dash of sugar.

Ingredients:

Fine rice flour	: 2 cups
Rice flour (puttu podi)	: 2 tablespoon
Coconut milk	: 2 ½ cups
Sesame oil	: 2 tablespoon
Yeast	: ¾ teaspoon
Sugar	: 2 tablespoons
Water	: 1 cup
Salt	: ½ teaspoon

Method of preparation:

- Bring to boil the rice flour (puttu podi) in water
- When it thickens like porridge set apart and allow to cool to room-temperature
- Add ½ teaspoon of sugar and 2 tablespoons of luke-warm water to the yeast and set aside to ferment
- Mix the fine rice flour, yeast and the thickened puttu podi & set apart for 5 hours for it to ferment
- When the mixture doubles add the coconut milk, salt and sugar
- Mix well together and set aside for 2 hours
- Heat the appam-chatti and brush lightly with oil
- Pour the mixture into the centre of the wok and swivel it once
- This ensures that the mixture is spread well, thinning at the edges
- Cover and cook for 2 minutes over low flame
- Do not turn it over and when the edges turn crispy brown, gently remove it from the appam-chatti
- Transfer to serving dish

KOZHY CURRY (CHICKEN 'N' CURRIED SAUCE)

Preparation Time: 10-15 min.   Cooking Time: 10-15 min.   Serves: 4-6

This is a delicious tangy dish and a favourite with the family. There are many variations of this recipe but this is my preferred version. It goes well with plain boiled rice and pappadums and is also an excellent side dish when served with idi appam, (string hoppers) appams, (rice cake) puttu (steamed rice cake) etc.

Ingredients:

Chicken	: 750 g (1.7 lbs.) cut into 10-cm (4 in.) cubes
Coconut oil or Ghee	: 8 teaspoons
Onions	: 1 cup finely sliced
Green chillies	: 6 Nos., slit
Red chilli powder	: 1 teaspoon
Coriander Powder	: 3 teaspoon
Turmeric powder	: 1 teaspoon
Garlic	: 8 cloves
Cashew nut pieces	: 2 teaspoons
Black Pepper Corns	: 10 Nos.
Cinnamon stick	: 2½ cm (1in) pieces
Cloves	: 8 Nos.
Star anis	: 2 Nos.
Tomatoes	: ½ cup chopped
Curds	: ½ cup
Salt	: 1 teaspoon or to taste
Water	: 1 cup

Method of preparation:

- Wet-grind the curry powders, cashew nuts, garlic and ¼ cup sliced onions.
- Smear above paste & salt on the chicken pieces and marinate for 10 minutes
- Sauté the onions lightly in the oil/ghee and remove.
- Add the spices one by one and when they sputter
- Add the chicken and fry well
- Add the tomatoes and fry till all water is evaporated
- Add ½ cup of water, close the vessel and cook over low flame till gravy is thick
- Add the curds, slit chillies and fried onions
- Add the sautéed onions and transfer to serving dish

MEEN MAPPAS (FISH 'N' CURRIED SAUCE)

Preparation Time: 10-15 min.   Cooking Time: 15-20 min.   Serves: 4-6

Meen mappas is a spicy fish preparation in thick curried sauce popular all over Kerala and is often served as a starter as well as the main dish. The spice levels maybe varied as per individual preferences. However, this preparation is not too hot albeit a little spicy and is served usually as a curry for rice, puttu (steamed rice-cake) or idiappam (string hoppers).

Ingredients:

Fish (seer)	: 900 g (2 lbs.) cleaned and sliced into 5 cm (2 in.) pieces
Coconut oil	: ¼ cup or 50 ml.
Onions	: 2 medium-sized; thinly sliced
Curry leaves	: 1½ stalk
Coconut milk	: 1 cup first extraction (thick)
Green chillies	: 5.sliced or slit
Fenugreek seeds	: ½ teaspoon
Red chilli powder	: 1½ teaspoon.
Turmeric powder	: ¼ teaspoon
Coriander powder	: 1½ teaspoon
Ginger	: 5 cm (1 in) cleaned and finely chopped
Garlic	: 10 cloves
Tomato	: 2 medium-sized ones - sliced
Mustard Seeds	: 1 pinch
Water	: 1 cup

Method of preparation:

- Mix the chilli, turmeric and coriander powders together in a little water
- Heat the oil in a pan and sprinkle the mustard seeds. When they sputter, add the fenugreek seeds
- Sauté the onions ginger, garlic & curry leaves and fry till the onions become transparent
- Add the soaked powders and fry 1-minute
- Add the sliced tomatoes and sauté finely
- Add water and bring to boil
- Add the sliced fish & salt and cook over low flame for few minutes till gravy thickens
- Pour in the coconut milk & bring to boil
- Transfer to a serving dish

29

MATTIRACHI PERALAN (BEEF 'N' SPICY SAUCE)

Preparation Time: 10-15 min. Cooking Time: 35-45 min. Serves: 6-7

Mattirachi curry is a hot and spicy beef preparation in thickly curried brownish sauce and one the favourites amongst especially the Christians of central Kerala. The spice levels maybe varied as per individual preferences. However, this preparation is best served slightly hot and tangy with practically everything including rice, kappa, (tapioca) idi appam, (string hoppers) appams, (rice cake) puttu (steamed rice cake) etc.

Ingredients:

Beef	: 900 g (2 lbs.) cleaned and chopped into 5-cm (2 in.) cubes
Coconut oil	: 3 tablespoons
Onions	: 2 big ones' finely chopped
Curry leaves	: 2 stalks
Green chillies	: 4 Nos., slit
Red chilli powder	: 2 teaspoons
Coriander Powder	: 1 teaspoon
Turmeric powder	: ½ teaspoon
Ginger	: 5 cm (1 in) cleaned and crushed
Garlic	: 10 cloves, crushed
Mustard Seeds	: 1 pinch
Aniseeds (perumgeerakam)	: ½ teaspoon
Cinnamon stick	: 2½ cm (1in) pieces
Cloves	: 3 Nos.
Star anis	: 2 Nos.
Tomatoes	: 2 Nos., chopped
Water	: ½ cup

Method of preparation:

- Soak the chilli, turmeric & coriander powders in a little water
- Powder aniseeds, cinnamon stick and cloves together
- Pressure cook the meat for 20 minutes adding water and salt.
- Separate stock from meat
- Heat the oil in a pan and add the mustard seeds and wait till they sputter
- Sauté the onions, green chillies curry leaves till the onions turn light brown
- Add the crushed ginger & garlic and finely sauté, and then lightly sauté the soaked powders
- Add the powdered spices & tomatoes and finely sauté
- Add the cooked meat to it and stir-fry for few minutes
- Add the stock and cook till the gravy becomes thick
- Transfer to serving dish

MEEN CURRY (FISH 'N' RED CURRY)

Preparation Time: 10-15 min. Cooking Time: 5-8 min. Serves: 4-6

Meen curry is a hot and spicy fish preparation in thickly curried red sauce and one of the all time favourites of every Malayali household. The spice levels maybe varied as per individual preferences. However, this preparation is best served slightly hot and tangy with rice, and is an extremely popular accompaniment with Kappa (tapioca).

Ingredients:

Fish	: 900 g (2 lbs.) cleaned and sliced into 5 cm (2 in.) pieces
Coconut oil	: 2 tablespoons
Mustard Seeds	: 1 pinch
Fenugreek seeds	: ½ teaspoon.
Shallots (small onions)	: 12 Nos. thinly sliced
Curry leaves	: 2 stalks
Red chilli powder	: 4 teaspoons, soaked in little water.
Turmeric powder	: ¼ teaspoon
Ginger	: 2.5 cm (½ in) cleaned and finely chopped
Garlic	: 5 cloves, finely chopped
Kokkum (Kudampul)	: 3 dried petals shredded into small piece and soaked in water
Water	: 1½ cups

Method of preparation:

- Heat the oil in a mann chatti or shallow clay pot
- Add the Mustard seeds, on sputtering add the fenugreek seeds to it
- Sauté the onions ginger, garlic & curry leaves and fry till the onions turns light brown
- Put the soaked chilli powder along with the turmeric powder and fry it
- Pour in the water, add the soaked Kokkum (kudampuli) and bring to boil
- Add the fish gently into the simmering gravy
- Add salt, cover the pot and cook for a few minutes over low flame till the oil separates
- Transfer to serving dish

KOZHY THENGA-VARUTHARACHATHU (CHICKEN 'N' FRIED COCONUT GRAVY)

Preparation Time: 10-15 min. Cooking Time: 20-25 min. Serves: 4-6

"Thenga Varutharachathu" literally translates to mean grated coconut fried and then ground into a fine paste. This wonderfully rich and creamy chicken preparation is perhaps a dish that is truly unique to Malayali households predominantly in central Kerala. I love to eat this with plain boiled rice, thick curds and Pappadams.

Ingredients:

Chicken	: 1kg (2 lbs.) chopped into 5-cm (2 in.) cubes
Coconut oil	: 2 tablespoon
Coconut	: 1½ cup (grated)
Shallots (small onions)	: 1 cup sliced in 2 pieces, 5Nos. finely chopped
Mustard Seeds	: 1 teaspoon
Green chillies	: 5 Nos., slit
Red chilli	: 16 Nos.
Coriander Powder	: 2 teaspoon
Turmeric powder	: ½ teaspoon
Garlic	: 4 cloves
Ginger	: 4 cm chopped
Aniseeds (perumgeerakam)	: ½ teaspoon
Cinnamon stick	: 2 cm (1in) pieces
Cloves	: 2 Nos.
Tomatoes	: 2 Nos. sliced
Curry Leaves	: 2 stalks
Salt	: To taste
Water	: 1 cup

Method of preparation:

- Fry the coconut, red chilli, coriander powder cinnamon, cloves, aniseed & curry leaves
- Keep stirring continuously and when the coconut turns brown set apart to cool
- Wet grind this mixture into a fine paste and set aside
- Cook the chicken, shallots, tomatoes, green chillies, ginger, garlic & salt till meat is tender
- Add the paste to the curry and boil till gravy thickens
- Heat the oil in a pan, add the mustard seeds
- When they crackle add the finely chopped shallots
- When the shallots turn brown add to the curry
- Transfer to serving dish

MEEN PEERA (FISH 'N' GRATED COCONUT)

Preparation Time: 10-15 min. Cooking Time: 5-8 min. Serves: 5-6

Meen Peera is a favoured Syrian Christian preparation using liberal quantity of grated coconut and flavoured with Kudampuli. This tangy preparation usually using small fishes such as fresh Matthi (sardines) or Podimeen (small fresh water fish) and tastes even better on the following day. This easy-to-cook and nourishing preparation is one of my father-in-law's favourites and is served as a side dish with rice.

Ingredients:

Fish	: 250 g (1 lbs.) cleaned and slit.
Crated Coconut	: ½ cup
Coconut oil	: 1 tablespoon
Shallots (small onions)	: 10 Nos. finely chopped
Curry leaves	: 2 stalks
Green chillies	: 5.sliced or slit
Turmeric powder	: ¼ teaspoon
Ginger	: 2.5 cm (½ in) finely chopped
Kokkum (Kudampuli)	: 2 dried petals.
Water	: ½cup

Method of preparation:

- Lightly crush the coconut, mix well with fingers, the Kokkum (kudampuli), onions, ginger, turmeric & green chillies along with salt and a little water in a shallow pot or mann chatti
- Add the fish and the curry leaves and pour in the water
- Cook for a few minutes till most of the water evaporates
- Add the oil and transfer to serving dish

AATTIRACHI BIRIYANI (LAMB BIRIYANI)

Preparation Time: 15-20 min. Cooking Time: 45-50 min. Serves: 7-8

This aromatic rice and meat preparation is usually served as a complete meal by itself especially on festive occasions such as weddings, birthday's etc, and is one of the favourites in our family.

Ingredients:

Lamb	: 1kg (2 lb.) lamb, cut into 5 cm (2 in.) cubes
Basmathi Rice	: 4 cups washed cleaned and drained.
Coconut oil	: 2 tablespoons
Ghee	: ½ cup
Onions	: 2 cups finely sliced
Green chillies	: 8 Nos.
Red chilli powder	: ½ teaspoon
Coriander Powder	: ½ teaspoon
Turmeric powder	: 1 teaspoon
Garlic	: ¼ cup
Ginger	: ¼ cup
Aniseeds (perumgeerakam)	: ½ teaspoon
Cinnamon stick	: 2½ cm (1in) pieces
Cloves	: 8 Nos.
Star anis	: 2 Nos.
Cardamom	: 10 Nos.
Tomatoes	: 1 cup finely chopped
Fresh lime juice	: 2 desert spoons
Coriander Leaves	: 1 handful
Mint Leaves	: 1 handful
Salt	: To taste

Method of preparation:

- Grind the ginger, garlic and green chillies
- Lightly fry cinnamon sticks, aniseeds, cloves, cardamom, and crush the spices together
- Fry 1 cup of onions till brown in the oil & ghee and remove
- Lightly sauté the remaining onions
- Add the ginger, garlic and green chillies to the onions and sauté well
- Add the spices, the curry powders and tomato and sauté well together till the oil separates
- Add the lamb and sauté till water evaporates
- Add 1 cup of water and the lime juice and cook over low flame
- When the meat is tender and the gravy thickens
- Add the coriander and mint leaves and set apart
- Boil 8 cups of salted water add the rice and cook till it is dry and just about done
- Drain the remaining water if any and set it apart
- Spread a portion of the rice in a large shallow vessel and add a portion of the lamb to it
- Repeat the process till both are mixed well together
- Sprinkle the browned onions on top and serve hot

MATHI CURRY (SARDINES 'N' MANGO CURRY)

Preparation Time: 10-15 min. Cooking Time: 5-8 min. Serves: 5-6

Sardines are found aplenty all along coastal Kerala and so is practically a staple part of almost every Malayali diet. Sardines with Mango are a popular variation especially with the Syrian Christian households in central Kerala. This tangy preparation is easy-to-cook and has a distinct and lingering flavour. It is usually served with rice and / or tapioca.

Ingredients:

Sardines	: 500 g (1.5 lbs.) cleaned and closely gashed.
Raw Mango pieces	: ½ mango cut into short slender pieces
Coconut oil	: 4 desert spoons
Shallots (small onions)	: 8Nos. Sliced, 2Nos finely chopped
Red Chilli	: Broken into 2 pieces
Garlic	: 2 cloves
Curry leaves	: 2 stalks
Green chillies	: 5 sliced or slit
Chilli Powder	: 1 teaspoon
Coriander Powder	: ½ teaspoon
Turmeric powder	: ½ teaspoon
Ginger	: 5 cm (1 in) cleaned and chopped
Grated Coconut	: 1½ cups
Mustard Seeds	: ½ teaspoon
Water	: 1 cups

Method of preparation:

- In a mann chatti boil the fish, ginger, onions, mango, chilli powder, for 10 minutes
- Grind the coconut, coriander powder, turmeric powder and garlic into a fine paste
- Add the paste to the thickened gravy in the mann chatti and bring to boil over low flame
- Heat the oil in a pan, add the mustard and on cracking
- Add the sliced onions, red chilli & curry leaves
- When the onions turn brown add to the curry
- Transfer to serving dish

THENGAPAL CHERTHA THARAVU (DUCK 'N' COCONUT MILK)

Preparation Time: 10-15 min. Cooking Time: 15-30 min. Serves: 4-6

This is a favourite preparation especially amongst the Malayalis who live in and around the banks of the backwaters of the mighty Vembanad Lake. Duck meat here has a flavour and aroma that is truly distinct to this region. When cooked in coconut milk the combination is simply irresistible and it is served on special occasions as a starter dish with appams. It is also one of my husband's favourite dishes and I learned it up from his mother.

Ingredients:

Duck	: 1kg, cut into 5cm pieces washed and drained
Potatoes	: 2 medium-sized; peeled and cubed
Coconut oil	: ¼ cup or 50 ml.
Onions	: 2 medium-sized; thinly sliced
Curry leaves	: 1½ stalk
Coconut milk	: 2 cups first extraction (thick)
Green chillies	: 3 sliced or slit
Tomatoes	: 2 medium-sized sliced
Red Chilli Powder	: 2 teaspoon
Coriander Powder	: 1 teaspoon
Turmeric Powder	: ¼ teaspoon
Black pepper powder	: 1 teaspoon.
Ginger	: 3 cm (0.5 in) crushed
Garlic	: 8 cloves crushed
Cinnamon stick	: 2½ cm (1 in) piece
Cloves	: 3
Cardamom	: 1 pod
Water	: 2½ cups

Method of preparation:

- Heat the oil in a heavy-bottomed pan
- Sauté the crushed cinnamon, cloves &cardamom for 1 minute
- Add the onions, ginger, green chillies & garlic
- When the onions turn transparent
- Add the curry powders and sauté
- Add the duck, salt, potatoes, tomatoes and sauté
- Pour in the water and cook till the meat is half done, add the thick coconut milk
- Reduce the heat and simmer for about 10 minutes till the meat is tender
- Transfer to a serving dish and garnish with curry leaves

MEEN MOILY (FISH 'N' COCONUT SAUCE)

Preparation Time: 10-15 min. Cooking Time: 15-20 min. Serves: 4-6

Meen mappas is a mildly spiced fish preparation in coconut milk and is a popular Syrian Christians of Central Kerala. It is usually served as a starter dish accompanied with Appams and is often served as a starter on festive occasions and is a favourite breakfast dish with my family, especially on Sundays. The recommended fish for this dish is Seer, (*Nenmeen*), Black Pomfret, (*Karimeen*) or Pomfret (*Aakoli*).

Ingredients:

Fish	: 500 g (1.5 lbs.) cleaned and sliced into 5 cm (2 in.) pieces
Coconut oil	: ¼ cup or 50 ml.
Onions	: 2 medium-sized; thinly sliced
Coconut milk	: 1 cup first extraction (thick) & 1½ cups second extraction
Green chillies	: 4 Nos. slit in two
Turmeric powder	: ¼ teaspoon
Ginger	: 3 cm (1 in) cleaned and finely chopped
Garlic	: 10 cloves
Tomato	: 2 medium-sized ones, cut into 4 pieces each
Cloves	: 2 Nos.
Cinnamon	: 2 cm, broken into 2 pieces
Pepper Powder	: ¼ teaspoon

Method of preparation:

- Heat the oil in a mann chatti or shallow clay pot and add cloves & cinnamon.
- When they sputter, add onions ginger, garlic & green chillies
- Sauté till the onions become transparent
- Lower the flame and add turmeric and salt to taste and mix well
- Place the fish pieces gently into the pot and mix together without breaking the fish slices
- Add the coconut milk (second extract) cover the pot and allow it to simmer till gravy thickens
- Add the sliced tomatoes and pepper powder and simmer for 2 minutes
- Add coconut milk (first extract) allowing it to only heat up & not boil
- Transfer to a serving dish

KOZHY MASALA (CHICKEN 'N' SPICEY SAUCE)

Preparation Time: 10-15 min. Cooking Time: 15 -20 min. Serves: 4-6

"Kozhy Masala" is how we refer to this delicious variation of the traditional chicken preparation as made by my mother. The spiciness of this dish is tempered down with two extracts of coconut milk, which also lends it an exotic flavour and colour. It can be served with the main course and is a wonderful accompaniment to just about anything from boiled rice to sliced bread.

Ingredients:

Chicken	: 1kg (2 lbs.) cut into 5-cm (2 in.) pieces
Coconut oil	: 4 tablespoon
Coconut milk	: 3 cups (1cup 1st extract, thick) & (2cups 2nd extract)
Potatoes	: 2 Nos. (boiled and cubed)
Onions	: 2 medium-sized thinly sliced
Shallots	: 10Nos.
Green chillies	: 5 Nos.
Black pepper corns	: 1 teaspoon
Red chillies	: 6 Nos. (to be ground without seeds)
Coriander Powder	: 1 teaspoon
Turmeric powder	: ½ teaspoon
Garlic	: 10 cloves
Ginger	: 3 cm
Aniseeds (perumgeerakam)	: ½ teaspoon
Cinnamon stick	: 2 cm
Cloves	: 2 Nos.
Star anis	: 2 Nos.
Cardamom	: 2 Nos.
Vinegar	: 2 teaspoons
Curry leaves	: 2 stalks
Salt	: To taste

Method of preparation:

- Powder aniseeds, cinnamon, cardamom, & cloves together
- Grind onions, shallots, garlic, ginger, green chillies, red chillies & pepper corns individually
- Finely sauté the onions and each of the ground ingredients individually
- Mix the sautéed items together along with the powdered spices and sauté again adding the chicken
- Add coconut milk 2nd extract, vinegar, curry leaves & salt
- Cook till meat is done and add the potatoes
- When gravy thickens, add coconut milk 1st extract
- Simmer for 2 minutes over low flame and transfer to serving dish

VARUTHA THARAVUKARI (DUCK ROAST 'N' SPICEY SAUCE)

Preparation Time: 10-15 min. Cooking Time: 20-30 min. Serves: 4-6

This is a special preparation of the roast duck in spicy red chillies. It is a wonderfully aromatic and colourful dish because of the dried red chillies. It is best served with boiled tapioca, appams or rice.

Ingredients:

Duck	: 1kg, cut into big pieces washed and drained
Potatoes	: 2 medium-sized; cut into thin long slices
Coconut oil	: ½ cup or 50 ml.
Onions	: 2 medium-sized; thinly sliced
Curry leaves	: 1½ stalk - chopped
Red chillies	: 10 Nos.
Turmeric Powder	: ¼ teaspoon
Black pepper corns	: 1 teaspoon.
Ginger	: 3 cm (0.5 in)
Garlic	: 10 cloves
Cinnamon stick	: 2½ cm (1 in) piece
Cloves	: 5 Nos.
Star anis	: 2 Nos.
Fresh Lime Juice	: 2 tablespoon
Water	: 2 cup

Method of preparation:

- Wet grind red chillies, peppercorns, garlic, ginger, cloves and cinnamon into paste
- Sauté the ground spices and turmeric powder in 1 tablespoon of oil
- Apply the sautéed spices evenly on the duck
- Add the curry leaves and water
- Cook till meat is done and the gravy thickens
- Separate the duck pieces from the gravy
- Heat the oil in a heavy-bottomed pan
- Fry the duck pieces till they turn brown
- Sauté the onions till it becomes brown
- Deep fry the potato slices adding a dash of salt
- Add the fried duck, onions, and lime juice to the gravy
- Transfer to serving dish and garnish the preparation with the fried potato

AATTIRACHI MAPPAS (MUTTON CURRY)

Preparation Time: 10-15 min. Cooking Time: 20-35 min. Serves: 4-6

This mutton dish cooked in coconut milk is mildly spiced and easy to make. It goes well with puttu, string hoppers or just plain rice very well. My mother-in-law makes this exceptionally well and I learned it up from her. We usually make it at home on special occasions and get-togethers.

Ingredients:

Mutton	: 1kg, cut into 5cm pieces washed and drained
Potatoes	: 3 medium-sized; peeled and cubed
Coconut oil	: ¼ cup or 50 ml.
Onions	: 2 medium-sized; thinly sliced
Curry leaves	: 1½ stalk
Coconut milk	: 2 cups
Green chillies	: 3 sliced or slit
Tomatoes	: 2 medium-sized sliced
Red Chilli Powder	: 2 teaspoon
Coriander Powder	: 4 teaspoon
Turmeric Powder	: ¼ teaspoon
Black pepper powder	: ½ teaspoon.
Ginger	: 4 cm (0.5 in) finely chopped
Garlic	: 10 cloves finely chopped
Cinnamon stick	: 2½ cm (1 in) powdered
Cloves	: 3 Nos. powdered
Salt	: To taste
Water	: 2½ cups

Method of preparation:

- Heat the oil & sauté the onions green chillies ginger and garlic together
- Add the pepper and curry powders and sauté
- Add tomatoes and sauté till they are done and then add the powdered spices
- Add the mutton & salt and stir fry for few minutes till water reduces
- Pour in the water and cook till the meat is half done and add the potatoes
- When the gravy is thick, add the coconut milk & curry leaves
- Reduce the heat and simmer for about 10 minutes till the meat is tender
- Transfer to serving dish

ULATHIYA IRACHI (BEEF FRY)

Preparation Time: 10-15 min. Cooking Time: 35-45 min. Serves: 6-7

Ulathiya Irachi is a fried beef dish of small boneless beef cubes that is twice cooked. It is first pressure cooked with spices and then fried with coconut and is a dish unique to Kerala. It practically stays fresh forever and seems to get tastier as you heat it each time. It compliments every main dish and my husband even has it for breakfast with puttu and bananas!

Ingredients:

Beef (boneless)	: 1 kg cleaned and cut into 2-cm cubes
Coconut oil	: ¼ cup
Coconut	: ½ cup thinly chopped into small pieces
Shallots	: 1 cup chopped
Onions	: 2 medium-sized chopped
Curry leaves	: 2 stalks
Red chilli powder	: 3 teaspoons
Coriander Powder	: 3 teaspoon
Turmeric powder	: ½ teaspoon
Ginger	: 5 cm (1 in) cleaned and crushed
Garlic	: 10 cloves, crushed
Aniseeds (perumgeerakam)	: ½ teaspoon
Cinnamon stick	: 2½ cm (1in) piece
Cloves	: 3 Nos.
Star anis	: 2 Nos.
Salt	: To taste

Method of preparation:

- Powder the aniseeds, cinnamon and cloves together
- Mix the powdered spices, garlic, ginger, coconut, shallots, curry powders & beef together
- Add salt to taste and pressure cook for15-20 minutes
- Cook over high flame with the lid open till water if any, evaporates
- Heat the oil in a pan and sauté the onions till it turns transparent
- Add curry leaves and meat — fry well, slowly over low flame
- Transfer to serving dish

KOZHY VARATHATHU (DEEP FRIED CHICKEN)

Preparation Time: 10-15 min. Cooking Time: 10-15 min. Serves: 4-5

Kozhy Varathathu is an all-time favourite with my boys. It is a great starter but could also be served as a main course with rice or buttery parotta. With zero onions and minimal spices, it is easy and fast to cook, especially when unexpected visitors drop in!

Ingredients:

Chicken	: 1 kg cleaned, cut into 5-cm pieces, washed and drained
Coconut oil	: ½ cup
Red chilli powder	: 2 teaspoons
Turmeric powder	: ½ teaspoon
Pepper	: 1 teaspoon
Ginger	: 5 cm (1 in)
Garlic	: 10 cloves,
Aniseeds (perumgeerakam)	: ½ teaspoon
Cinnamon stick	: 2½ cm (1in) piece
Cloves	: 3 Nos.
Lime juice	: 2 tablespoon
Salt	: To taste

Method of preparation:

- Powder the aniseeds, cinnamon and cloves together
- Grind the ginger & garlic into a fine paste
- Mix the powdered spices, garlic, ginger, curry powders, lime juice
- Marinate the chicken well with the mixture & refrigerate for ½ hour or more
- Heat the oil in a pan and deep fry the marinated chicken with the lid closed
- Transfer to serving dish when both side are evenly brown

IRACHI ACCHAR (BEEF PICKLE)

Preparation Time: 10-15 min. Cooking Time: 35-45 min. Serves: 8-10

Pickled beef goes well with every main dish lending a distinct flavour and colour. Kindly note that for the recipe given below, the pickle should always be bottled and refrigerated as only minimal oil and zero preservatives are used. Take care not to use wet spoons when serving the pickle.

Ingredients:

Beef	: 1 kg cleaned, cut into 2-cm pieces, washed and drained
Coconut oil	: 1 cup
Gingili Oil	: 1 cup
Red chilli powder	: 3 tablespoon
Turmeric powder	: ½ teaspoon
Ginger	: 5 cm (1 in)
Garlic	: 15 cloves
Fenugreek	: 1 teaspoon
Mustard	: 1 teaspoon
Asafoetida	: 1 teaspoon
Curry leaves	: 2 stalks
Vinegar	: ½ cup
Water	: ½ cup
Salt	: To taste

Method of preparation:

- Pressure cook the beef with salt and turmeric powder till it is just about done
- Cook over high flame with the lid open to vaporise remaining water if any
- Deep fry the meat in coconut oil and set apart
- Crush the ginger & garlic
- Boil the vinegar and water and set apart
- Heat the oil, add the mustard and fenugreek
- When they crackle, add the ginger, garlic, curry leaves and fry
- Remove from flame & immediately add the curry powders
- Add the fried beef along with the boiled vinegar/water
- Bottle and transfer to refrigerator when cool

57

MEEN ACCHAR (PICKLED FISH)

Preparation Time: 10-15 min. Cooking Time: 25-30 min. Serves: 7-10

For pickling the recommended fish is either seer or tuna. The best thing I like about this pickle is that it is a great substitute for fish dish during meals. Kindly note that for the recipe given below, the pickle should always be bottled and refrigerated as only minimal oil and zero preservatives are used. Take care not to use wet spoons when serving the pickle.

Ingredients:

Fish	: 1 kg cleaned, sliced into 2-cm pieces
Coconut oil	: 1 cup
Gingili Oil	: 1 cup
Red chilli powder	: 3 tablespoon
Pepper powder	: 1 teaspoon
Turmeric powder	: ½ teaspoon
Ginger	: 5 cm (1 in) chopped
Garlic	: 15 cloves chopped
Fenugreek	: 1 teaspoon
Mustard	: 1 teaspoon
Asafoetida	: 1 teaspoon
Vinegar	: ½ cup
Curry leaves	: 2 stalks
Salt	: To taste

Method of preparation:

- Marinate the fish with pepper powder, turmeric powder and salt to taste
- Deep fry in coconut oil and set apart
- Heat the gingili oil, add fenugreek and mustard
- When they sputter, add the ginger, garlic, curry leaves and fry
- Remove from flame & immediately add the chilli & asafoetida powders
- Add the fried fish along with vinegar
- Bottle and transfer to refrigerator when cool

MEEN VARATHATHU (FRIED FISH)

Preparation Time: 10-15 min. Cooking Time: 10-15 min. Serves: 3-5

You could use any firm-fleshed fish to fry in this manner. I usually use Pomfret (Aakoli), Pearl Spot, (Karimeen) or Seer. Almost any kind of fish can be fried in the below given manner. However, ensure that the fish is fresh and sliced into medium pieces

Ingredients:

Fish	: ½ kg
Coconut oil	: ¼ cup
Red chilli powder	: 1 teaspoon
Pepper Corns	: 1 teaspoon
Turmeric powder	: ½ teaspoon
Ginger	: 2½ cm (0.5 in)
Garlic	: 5 cloves
Vinegar	: 1 teaspoon
Salt	: To taste

Method of preparation:

- Grind the pepper corns, chilli, turmeric powders, salt ginger and garlic along with vinegar
- Marinate the fish with the ground paste
- Fry in coconut oil
- Transfer to serving dish

MEEN POLLICHATHU (FISH 'N' BANANA LEAF)

Preparation Time: 10-15 min. Cooking Time: 10-15 min. Serves: 8-9

Meen Pollichathu is a truly mouth-watering delicacy and was a very popular dish especially of yesteryears when people had the time and the patience to make such exotic preparations to savour the natural flavours of superb fish. If banana leaves are difficult to obtain, aluminium leaves work almost as well. I recommend Pearl Spot, (Karimeen) or Pomfret for this dish. Make horizontal deep cuts on the fish so that the spice paste permeates the flesh.

Ingredients:

Fish	: 1 kg
Banana Leaves	: 8 Nos. cut into pieces large enough to wrap a whole fish
Coconut oil	: ½ cup
Red chilli	: 10 Nos.
Onions	: 2 Nos. thinly sliced
Tomato	: 2Nos.chopped into small pieces
Pepper Corns	: 1 teaspoon
Turmeric powder	: ½ teaspoon
Ginger	: 2½ cm (0.5 in)
Garlic	: 10 cloves
Salt	: To taste

Method of preparation:

- Grind the pepper corns, chilli, turmeric powder, salt, ginger and garlic
- Heat 2 tablespoons of oil in a frying pan
- Sauté the onions till they become transparent
- Add the ground paste and sauté well
- Add the tomatoes and cook till they are done
- Remove from flame and keep aside till it attains room temperature
- Apply the paste evenly on the fish
- Run the banana leaves over a flame to make them pliable
- Apply a little oil on the banana leaves with a muslin cloth
- Wrap each fish individually in the banana leaves and sew the edges of the leaf with tooth picks
- Roast on a shallow pan or griddle for 2 to 5 minutes flipping over at even intervals
- Alternatively you can steam the wrapped fish in a steamer for 5 to 7 minutes
- Transfer to serving dish

CHEMMEN CURRY (PRAWNS 'N' GROUND COCONUT)

Preparation Time: 10-15 min. Cooking Time: 10-15 min. Serves: 4-5

Chemmeen or prawns, especially fresh from the backwaters of Kerala have a unique flavour all their own. Any, which way you make them they are irresistible. This is a preparation in ground coconut with thick gravy that is simply fantastic with just pain rice or Kappa Puzhingyathu (boiled tapioca).

Ingredients:

Prawns	:	250 gms cleaned and drained
Coconut oil	:	2 tablespoons
Grated coconut	:	1 cup
Red chilli	:	2 Nos. chopped
Shallots	:	4 Nos. - (2 Nos. sliced & 2 Nos. to be ground)
Green Chilli	:	4 Nos. slit
Curry leaves	:	2 stalks
Kokkum (kudampuli)	:	2 dried petals shredded into small piece and soaked in water
Chilli powder	:	½ teaspoon
Coriander powder	:	1 teaspoon
Turmeric powder	:	½ teaspoon
Mustard	:	½teaspoon
Ginger	:	2 cm thinly sliced
Garlic	:	2 cloves
Water	:	1 cup
Salt	:	To taste

Method of preparation:

- Grind together the coconut, garlic, coriander powder, shallots & turmeric powder into a fine paste
- In a mann chatti or shallow clay pot mix the prawns, chilli powder, kokum, green chilli, ginger and salt
- Add water and cook for 10 minutes
- Add the ground paste and simmer for 5 minutes
- Heat oil in a pan
- Add the mustard, and when they sputter
- Add sliced shallots, red chilli and curry leaves and fry till they become brown
- Add to the curry and transfer to serving dish

CHEMMEN MASALA (PRAWNS MASALA)

Preparation Time: 10-15 min. Cooking Time: 10-15 min. Serves: 4-5

This is an easy-to-make dry preparation of prawns that doubles as an excellent snack as well as a side dish with the main course.

Ingredients:

Prawns	: ½ kg cleaned and drained
Coconut oil	: 4 tablespoons
Onions	: 2 medium-sized thinly sized
Tomato	: 2 medium ones finely chopped
Chilli Powder	: 2 teaspoons
Curry leaves	: 2 stalks
Coriander powder	: ½ teaspoon
Turmeric powder	: ½ teaspoon
Garlic	: 7 cloves finely chopped
Salt	: To taste

Method of preparation:

- Marinate the prawns with the turmeric and salt
- Boil for 10 minutes till water evaporates
- Heat the oil in a pan
- Sauté the onions till they are transparent and the add the curry leaves
- Add the garlic and sauté well.
- Add the tomatoes plus the curry powders and sauté together till all the water has evaporated
- Add the prawns and sauté over low flame till it becomes dry
- Transfer to serving dish

CHEERA CURRY (SPINACH 'N' COCONUT MILK)

Preparation Time: 10-15 min. Cooking Time: 10min. Serves: 4-5

Cheera is one of the most nutritious and one the most easily available leafy vegetable here in Kerala. We have both the green spinach as well as the red. It is an excellent accompaniment to rice, chappathi etc. This dish was my father's favourite and my mother makes it at home very often.

Ingredients:

Red Cheera	: 3 cups of tender leaves (do not chop them), washed & drained
Coconut oil	: 4 tablespoons
Coconut milk	: 2 ½ cups
Shallots	: 20 Nos. crushed
Red Chilli	: 5 Nos. crushed
Garlic	: 6 cloves crushed
Salt	: To taste

Method of preparation:

- Heat the oil in a pan
- Add the crushed ingredients and sauté well
- Add Cheera along with salt and sauté
- Cover the vessel and cook for 2 to 3 minutes
- Add the coconut milk
- Simmer for few minutes without bringing it to boil
- Transfer to serving dish

VENDEKKA VARATHATHU (ROAST LADY'S FINGER)

Preparation Time: 10-15 min. Cooking Time: 10min. Serves: 4-5

This is yet another speciality dish from my mother's kitchen. Make sure you use very tender lady's fingers only. I love this best with plain rice and chicken curry.

Ingredients:

Lady's Finger	: 10 Nos. to be slit without splitting
Coconut oil/Ghee	: ¼ cup
Shallots	: 6 Nos.
Pepper corns	: 1½ tablespoon
Cinnamon	: 2 cm
Cloves	: 4 Nos.
Aniseeds	: ½ teaspoon
Salt	: To taste

Method of preparation:

- Grind shallots, pepper corns, cinnamon, cloves and aniseed well together
- Apply the mixture with salt well within and outside the lady's fingers'
- Put in the steamer for 2 to 3 minutes
- Heat the oil/ghee in a pan
- Add the steamed lady's fingers' and sauté for 2 minutes
- Transfer to serving dish

AVIAL (MIXED VEGETABLES 'N' COCONUT)

Preparation Time: 10-15 min. Cooking Time: 10-15 min. Serves: 5-6

Avial is delightfully non-spicy vegetable side dish that is an excellent accompaniment to rice along with the relatively more spicy meat and/or fish dishes. Avial is indeed an "all Kerala" traditional vegetarian preparation which is a must-have at every Sadhya or feast and it is one delicacy which is every bit as nourishing as well as tasty. This is an all-time favourite of my father-in-law who loves it best with red fish curry.

Ingredients:

Carrot
Raw Bananas
Yam
Potato
Cucumber
Aubergine (Brinjal)
Drumsticks
Snake gourd
The above vegetables should be sliced evenly into 6cm or 2-inch pieces totalling 3 cups

Onions	: 2 large (sliced)
Tomato	: 3 sliced
Coconut	: 3 cups (grated)
Garlic	: 2 cloves
Coconut oil	: 1½ tablespoon
Curry leaves	: 2 stalks
Green Chillies	: 7 Nos. slit
Turmeric Powder	: ½ teaspoon
Chilli Powder	: ½ teaspoon
Cumin Seeds	: ½ teaspoon

Method of preparation:

- Coarsely grind the grated coconut, cumin seeds & garlic
- Bring to boil the mixed vegetables, onions, salt turmeric & chilli powders in 1½ cups of water
- Add tomatoes and cook well
- Add the coarsely ground paste and cook for 2 minutes continually stirring
- Add the oil & curry leaves and transfer to serving dish

73

PAVAYKKA THORAN (BITTER GOURED 'N' GRATED COCONUT)

Preparation Time: 8-10 min. Cooking Time: 10-15 min. Serves: 3-4

Pavaykka Thoran is a unique dish in that its bitterness actually supplements the flavour. It is a very tasty accompaniment with rice, buttermilk and fish fry. It is one of my husband's favourites and we make it often at home as this is one of the few vegetables that he loves.

Ingredients:

Bitter Gourd	: 1 sliced into thin pieces
Coconut	: 1 cup grated
Green chillies	: 5 Nos. (sliced thin)
Shallots	: 12 Nos. (sliced thin)
Coconut oil	: 1 tablespoon
Curry leaves	: 2 stalks
Salt	: To taste
Water	: 2 tablespoons

Method of preparation:

- Mix all the ingredients together in a mann chatti
- Cook over low flame till water evaporates
- Add the coconut oil, stir well
- Transfer to serving dish

PAAL PAYASM (RICE 'N' MILK DESSERT)

Palpayasm is a traditional dessert made and served especially on occasions such as birthdays and for the festival of Onam - an annual festival celebrated all over Kerala in the month September. This is simply delicious when served chilled.

Ingredients:

Basmathi Rice	: ¼ cup
Milk	: 4 cups
Sugar	: 1 cup
Water	: 1 cup
Ghee	: 1 tablespoon
Cashew Nuts	: ¼ cup broken
Cardamom	: 3Nos. powdered

Method of preparation:

- Pressure cook all ingredients (excepting ghee and cashew nuts) for ½ hour
- Heat the ghee in a shallow wok and fry the cashew nuts till they turn light brown
- Add the pressure cooked mixture and stir together
- Transfer to serving dish and serve warm or chilled

PAYARU PAYASAM (GREEN GRAM 'N'- MILK DESSERT)

Parippu payasam is yet another milk based traditional dessert and this is how my grandmother used to make it for us when we used to visit her during our holidays.

Ingredients:

Green Gram Dal	: 100 gms
Jaggery	: 150 gms
Sago (chowwari)	: 3 teaspoons
Coconut	: 3 tablespoon, cut into small pieces
Sultanas (Kishmis)	: 2 tablespoon
Coconut Milk	: 1st Extract 1 cup & 2nd extract 2 cups
Ghee	: 3 tablespoon
Cashew Nuts	: ¼ cup broken
Cardamom	: ½ teaspoon powdered
Water	: 3 cups

Method of preparation:

- Bring the jaggery to boil in 1 cup of water
- Stir well and cook till jaggery melts and begins to thicken and set apart
- Fry the Green gram lightly till it turns brownish
- Pressure cook the fried Green gram and the Sago for 10 minutes in 2 cups of water
- Mash the Green gram and Sago well and add 2nd extract of coconut milk and jaggery syrup
- Bring to boil stirring at regular intervals till the mixture thickens
- Add the 1st extract of coconut milk and stir in the cardamom powder
- Remove from flame and set apart
- Heat the ghee and fry the coconut pieces well and set apart
- Fry the Sultanas in the ghee till it puffs up and set apart
- Fry the cashew nuts also in ghee till they turn brown
- Add all fried ingredients and the remaining ghee to the payasam
- Transfer it to serving dish and serve warm or chilled

Publish and Sell your books Worldwide !

DEE BEE BOOKS has a wealth of experience in producing colorful, well designed cook books, Picture books and Brochures. Dee Bee books provide full range of service, from concept through to printing, marketing and distribution.

More information:
salimpushpanath@gmail.com
www.salimpushpanath.com

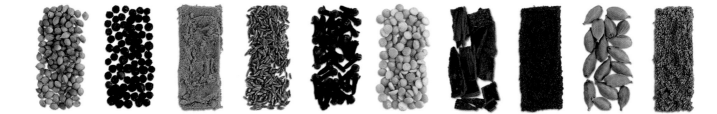

Buy our publications on-line from www.amazon.com